T0193751

PASSOVER HAGGADAH

Dr. Dickie (Richard) Marks

Copyright © 2023 by Dr. Dickie (Richard) Marks. 842856

All rights reserved. No part of this book may be reproduced or transmitted in any form or by any means, electronic or mechanical, including photocopying, recording, or by any information storage and retrieval system, without permission in writing from the copyright owner.

To order additional copies of this book, contact:
Xlibris
844-714-8691
www.Xlibris.com
Orders@Xlibris.com

ISBN: Softcover   978-1-6698-6293-2
         EBook   978-1-6698-6292-5

Print information available on the last page

Rev. date: 01/30/2023

THE SEDER BEGINS...

Leader reads:

We gather tonight wearing dresses or pants;
With Mommies, or Daddies, or uncles, or aunts;
Or cousins, or friends, or with grandpas or grannies;
Or people who shouldn't be alone; or with nannies.
To tell a short story; we'll have to eat later.
It's Passover night, so let's get down and seder!

We start giving thanks to the God who has made us;
Who must be real smart; to invent and create us.
To Whom we're all equal, in high heels or sandals.
But might see us better if we light some candles.

*Leader may explain that the first seder ever held was to celebrate the
first anniversary of our freedom from slavery in Egypt.*

*Leader may additionally explain that the significance of candle lighting is the symbolic
giving of brightness and spiritual illumination to a celebratory event.*

To accompany candle lighting, Leader and participants recite together:

Blessing #1

בָּרוּךְ אַתָּה יְיָ אֱלֹהֵינוּ מֶלֶךְ הָעוֹלָם אֲשֶׁר קִדְּשָׁנוּ בְּמִצְוֹתָיו וְצִוָּנוּ
לְהַדְלִיק נֵר שֶׁל (שַׁבָּת וְשֶׁל) יוֹם טוֹב.

*Baruch Atah Adonai, Eloheinu melech ha'olam, asher kid'shanu b'mitzvotav, v'tzivanu l'hadlik
ner, shel (Shabbat v'shel) Yom Tov.*

We praise You, Adonai our God, Ruler of the Universe, Who makes us holy by Your
mitzvot and commands us to light the (Sabbath and) festival lights.

Leader may explain that the following prayer is in honor of celebration:

Blessing #2:

בָּרוּךְ אַתָּה יְיָ אֱלֹהֵינוּ מֶלֶךְ הָעוֹלָם שֶׁהֶחֱיָנוּ וְקִיְּמָנוּ וְהִגִּיעָנוּ
לַזְּמַן הַזֶּה.

*Baruch Atah Adonai, Eloheinu melech ha'olam, shehecheyanu, v'kiy'manu, v'higianu, lazman
hazeh.*

We praise You, Adonai our God, Ruler of the Universe, Who has kept us
alive and well so that we can celebrate this special time.

Leader reads:

Besides making people, God made trees and vines;
And grapes, which, if squeezed right, make something called wine.
Most grown-ups at seders will drink it four times.
While kiddies use grape juice; which works out just fine!

Leader may explain that wine is part of the proceedings for two reasons. First, wine is meant to symbolize joy at a celebration. Second and more specific for Passover, wine is considered a drink enjoyed by royals; and, like our theoretical reclining versus sitting in upright postures during this seder (asked later with The Four Questions), taking on customs usually associated with royals is meant to reflect our elation upon gaining freedom from Egyptian slavery.

Before drinking the first cup of wine, Leader and participants recite together:

בָּרוּךְ אַתָּה יְיָ אֱלֹהֵינוּ מֶלֶךְ הָעוֹלָם בּוֹרֵא פְּרִי הַגָּפֶן.

Baruch Atah Adonai, Eloheinu melech ha'olam, borei p'ri hagafen.

We praise You, Adonai our God,
Ruler of the Universe,
Who creates the fruit of the vine.

Leader shows the seder plate and reads:

Now look at this plate. I know this is an egg.
And a yucky old bone — kind of looks like a leg!
There's honey with apples and nuts that look yummy.
But this is for show; not to stuff in your tummy.

Yet each of those things are put there for a reason:
They all tell us something this holiday season:
Of people whose lives were no fun; they were bitter.
Of times before i-phones, and facebook, and twitter.
Our ancestors — grandparents' parents, and more
All worked for mean bullies. Though tired and sore
They were pushed to their limits; and drained to the core.

Leader begins by highlighting karpas; explaining that the salt water, in which they are soon to be dipped, replicates the tears of ancestors, yet the greens themselves, if not dipped in the salty brine, would otherwise represent symbols of spring and renewal, and therefore hope.

The bitter things here on the plate bring us tears,
As wept by our forefathers all through the years
They made mortar and bricks; and that mix called charoses
Relives those hard days before freedom, and Moses.

Leader indicates charoses; symbolizing the brick and mortar mix our ancestors were forced to make during their period of enslavement.

An egg was a gift to our leaders, called priests.

Leader indicates the beitzah; the boiled egg given as gifts to spiritual leaders in ancient times.

Maror recalls times Jews were treated like beasts.

Leader indicates the maror; bitter herbs meant to reflect bitterness of our enslavement.

They endured 'til the night Egypt's stronghold was broken.
The lamb bone then saved them once God's word was spoken.

Leader indicates the zeroa, the lamb shank bone. Marking the doorposts of Jewish homes with blood on the tip of a lamb shank bone repelled the Angel of Death from the homes of those so protected, saving them from God's tenth and final plague — death of the first born.

We'll soon tell a story to help understand.
But before getting started, have we washed our hands?

Leader may explain that he/she will ceremonially rinse their own hands to represent washing of all those present. Leader may further explain that this ceremonial hand washing is an act of cleansing, therefore of health assuring sanitation. The washing of hands, however, has an even deeper meaning; one of spiritual as well as bodily purification, in that the rabbis of the time, then called priests (as just alluded to in the preceding verse), washed their hands before performing rituals or giving blessings.

Following the ceremonial hand washing, Leader asks participants to take a piece of karpas (usually a green vegetable, such as celery or parsley), dip it in salt, and eat. Leader may remind participants of the explanation given earlier of the significance of the green vegetables — spring, renewal, and hope - and the neutering of such hope by the tear-like salt water in which they are dipped.

Leader reads, while dipping takes place:

Now we dip veggies, in water quite salted.
Like tears shed before our enslavement was halted;
When we were abused, set upon, and assaulted
Before we were saved by Almighty Exalted.

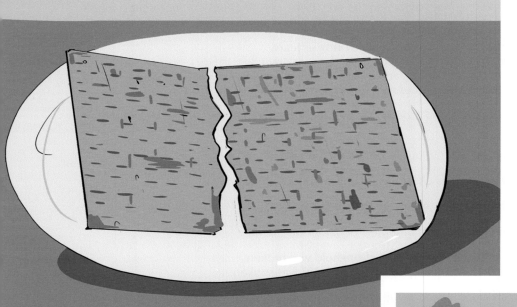

Following the dipping of the karpas, Leader holds up the matzoh and may explain that matzoh is part of the Passover celebration for many reasons: The most commonly stated reason is that it was in the best interest of the Jews, once freed from Egyptian slavery, to leave as soon as possible. They did not have time to wait for their bread to rise. Others add that matzoh was considered "bread" for the poor. This was due to the extra expense of the additional flour needed to make the bread rise as well as symbolic; in that the flatness of the matzoh reflected humility, whereas the fullness of leavened bread suggested arrogance.

Leader, or next participant, reads:

On Passover we're not supposed to eat bread;
So we munch these huge crackers called matzoh instead. The reason's because long before we had cars,
Before we sent spaceships to Venus or Mars, our ancestors had to ride
donkeys or camels, or horses, or oxen, or other tough mammals.
They didn't have the time for French toast or grilled cheese. They settled for crunchy big munchies, like these.

I'll break off a piece, and we'll play hide and seek.
When I tiptoe away close your eyes........Don't you peak!

Leader hides the afikomen, after which follows what is perhaps the best known of all the customary aspects of a Passover seder: The asking of what has become known simply as:

The Four Questions

Leader may explain that the traditional four questions which follow, each in reference to various customs specific to seder celebrations, are asked by the youngest person present at the seder who is comfortable in their ability to read.

Leader, other participant, or more commonly the candidate who will be asking the four questions, begins by reading/ singing:

מַה־נִּשְׁתַּנָּה הַלַּיְלָה הַזֶּה מִכָּל־הַלֵּילוֹת!

Mah nishtanah halailah hazeh mikol haleilot!

How different this night is from all other nights!

Following that commentary, which itself is truly a stand alone statement, and not one of the well established four questions, the youngest literate person present takes center stage for this portion of the seder, and recites the time honored four questions:

The four questions may be asked in Hebrew, in English (English translations are below the Hebrew transliterations), in verse (below the Hebrew script), or in any combination with which the Leader and participants feel comfortable and appropriate for those in attendance.

שֶׁבְּכָל־הַלֵּילוֹת אָנוּ אוֹכְלִין חָמֵץ וּמַצָּה, הַלַּיְלָה הַזֶּה כֻּלּוֹ מַצָּה.

Sheb'chol haleilot anu ochlin chametz u'matzah. Halailah hazeh, kulo matzah.

שֶׁבְּכָל־הַלֵּילוֹת אָנוּ אוֹכְלִין שְׁאָר יְרָקוֹת, הַלַּיְלָה הַזֶּה מָרוֹר.

Sheb'chol haleilot anu ochlin she'ar yirakot. Halailah hazeh maror.

שֶׁבְּכָל־הַלֵּילוֹת אֵין אָנוּ מַטְבִּילִין אֲפִלּוּ פַּעַם אֶחָת, הַלַּיְלָה הַזֶּה שְׁתֵּי פְעָמִים.

Sheb'chol haleilot ein anu matbilin afilu pa'am echat,. Haleilah hazeh sh'tei f'amim.

שֶׁבְּכָל־הַלֵּילוֹת אָנוּ אוֹכְלִין בֵּין יוֹשְׁבִין וּבֵין מְסֻבִּין, הַלַּיְלָה הַזֶּה כֻּלָּנוּ מְסֻבִּין.

Sheb'chol haleilot anu ochlin bein yoshvin u'vein m'subin. Halailah hazeh kulanu m'subin.

Four questions are asked:
Why not bread? Why eat matzoh?
And why eat maror, when we know there are lotsa'
Good veggies.......like corn, or like beans, or like rice.
And why should we lean, not sit upright and nice?

On all other nights we eat bread or matzah. Why tonight only matzah?
On all other nights we eat all kinds of vegetables. Why tonight only maror?
On all other nights we do not dip any vegetables even once. Why now twice?
On all other nights we sit upright. Why should we lean on pillows tonight?

If Leader chooses to actually address each of the questions, he/she may briefly remind participants of what had just been explained about why matzoh is eaten at Passover, and therefore at seder celebrations; further explaining how the vegetable chosen to represent maror is specifically meant to be bitter, made all the more distasteful by dipping it in salt water. The unpleasant taste recalls the bitterness of enslavement. Leaning is in celebration of our ancestors' newfound freedom, meant to imitate the reclining postures that royals often assumed during meals. In addition to, or instead of, those literal answers given to the questions just asked, the questions could be answered more briefly in verse.

Leader, or next participant, summarizes the answers:

THE PASSOVER STORY

The answers relate to the stories we're telling;
No taco stands, burgers; nobody was selling
Cheese pizzas, or cupcakes, or chilled soup de jour.
And matzoh was cheap; it was bread for the poor.
Maror dipped in salt is a bad tasting treat;
Reminds us of sweat from the overworked feet
Our ancestors slaved on, with backbreaking toil.
We lean toasting freedom; the posture of royals!

Leader continues, or next participant reads:

Four children ask more. The first one is wise:
"That powerful Being we can't see in the skies—
What means all God tells us?" To which one replies
In a scholarly way. Then the wicked one sighs,
Sneering nastily, "What means this service to <u>you</u>?"
Though he may not admit it, he's part of it too.
The simple son asks, "What is all this about?"
We sweetly explain then how God got us out.
And last there's the baby; just asks to be fed.
We burp her and change her, and put her to bed.

Leader continues, or next participant reads: Moses' voice should be delivered with force and absolute conviction; Pharoah's with arrogant amusement:

Now time for the story of Pharoah and Moses:
The ruler of Egypt quite wrongly supposes
The Israelites, who had been working as slaves
While building the pyramids, living in caves
Would stay on forever; keep working for free;
Until Moses said, "No! You're dealing with me!
I'm one with my people, and you'll let them go!"
The Pharoah laughed loudly, and asked, "Is that so?
And why, Mr. Moses, please kindly explain,
Would I let all my plans burble right down the drain?"

Leader continues, or next participant reads: Moses with a warning tone in his voice:

But Moses was serious and hardly amused;
Empowered by God, he'd get Pharoah enthused.
Determined; one plague at a time, very slow,
Eventually Pharoah would "Let my folks go!"
"Are you certain, dear Pharoah, your answer is no?
There's no way at all that my people can go?"

Leader continues, or next participant reads: Pharoah with a dismissive and mocking tone:

"I'm sure, Moses, I won't be doing what you'd like.
So save yourself time now, and go take a hike!"

Leader continues: or next participant reads: Moses asking God with authority!

'Twas clear then to Moses just what must be done.
"Let's bring on the plagues, God." From then, one by one,
The Almighty's fury descended from heaven.
The tenth was the clincher — it wouldn't take eleven.

Traditionally, immediately after each plague is named, each seder participant dips the tip of their finger into their wine or wine equivalent, and taps that drop of wine onto their plate. Each dip and tap takes only two to three seconds, and the text below indicates when those brief pauses in the reading of the plagues should be taken. If the Leader wishes to preserve the poetic cadence, and is familiar with the text, the following is best read by the Leader:

The first turned the water to blood (pause); second — frogs (pause)!
The third featured lice (pause); then came rampaging hogs (pause).
The fifth killed off cattle (pause); the sixth - massive sores (pause).
Then hail (pause), then locusts (pause), then darkness (pause).
"No more!!
I think I'm convinced." Pharoah started to fold.
Advisors advised: "Sir, you'll look weak and old."
So he folded his arms, and looked Mose' in the eye.
Insisted, "Slaves stay! Now get lost; and good bye!"

Leader continues, or next participant reads darkly, with foreboding:

Response was immediate from Moses that night:
"Pharoah, I warn you. The tenth will bring fright
The likes of which never has been in your sight."

Leader continues, or next participant reads: Pharoah's first line with arrogance; second line with profound grief; then finally Pharoah's shouts with barely contained vehemence and anger:

"Let's bring it on, Moses; let's see what
you've got." A sad day.......
All first born were dead on the spot.

* * * * * * * * * * * * * * *

Pharoah shrieked, "Moses, take every last soul.
Get out of my sight! You've accomplished your goal."

Leader continues, or next participant reads: Last line with venom and vengeance:

As the newly freed masses trudged on towards the sea
Sad Pharoah wept; his firstborn limp on his knee.
Heart hardened, unwisely, he then changed his mind;
Commanding his troops, "Kill each one that you find."

Leader continues, or next participant reads: Last line a battle cry to inspire the troops:

While Moses and all of his people stood staring
At waves topped with whitecaps,
Egyptians were bearing down on their
position; with arrows and spears.
"Our firstborn are gone due to them. They'll pay dear!"

Leader continues, or next participant reads: With wonderment and awe:

Then Moses looked up at the heavens and pleaded
For safety. God then gave him just what he needed:
The sea waters parted, allowing the nation
Free passage across.........muddy path to salvation.

15

Leader continues, or next participant reads: First four lines spoken with mounting excitement; then with a changed voice suggesting finality and solemn acceptance of Divine intervention:

As Israelites stepped up on the opposite shore
The well armed Egyptians pursued with a roar.
They followed the path made just minutes before
Taking arrows from quivers to even the score.

Then the Lord showed his wrath — slammed the watery door.....
And the army of Egypt existed no more.

Leader continues, or next participant reads:

After roaming the desert for forty full years,
The Israelites, knowing both heartache and tears,
Did arrive at the land they'd been promised, at last; Yet Moses, now
aged, knew his time had passed.
He'd done all that God asked; more than ample reward.
They'd cross Jordan without him, a stream he couldn't ford.
They would make the land flourish, bring honey and milk.
Would establish their roots, so that all of their ilk
For time immemorial, as The Covenant knows,
Would give comfort to God for the people He chose.

Leader reads:

In honor and praise of the freedom God gave us
To leave the taskmasters who so long enslaved us
We toast once again the Almighty in heaven
Before breaking bread; though the bread be unleavened.

Blessing #4: Second cup of wine

בָּרוּךְ אַתָּה יְיָ אֱלֹהֵינוּ מֶלֶךְ הָעוֹלָם בּוֹרֵא פְּרִי הַגָּפֶן.

Baruch Atah Adonai, Eloheinu melech ha'olam,, borei p'ri hagafen.

We praise You, Adonai our God, Ruler of the Universe, Who creates the fruit of the vine.

"Sandwich",

Dinner,

Afikomen Time

Leader may explain the symbolism of a Hillel sandwich:

The "Hillel sandwich" is made of matzoh and maror. In the days of the Temple in Jerusalem, Rabbi Hillel would eat a sandwich of matzoh and maror, a bitter herb, topped with a slice of sacrificial lamb. Since there is no sacrifice involved, the sandwich we make tonight, meant to commemorate the awful taste of bondage and slavery, is nowadays made only with matzoh — bread of the poor - and maror — symbolic of bitterness once suffered.

Leader then reads:

Now on that unleavened crisp treat, the matzoh,
We pucker our lips, the maror giving lotsa'
Good reasons that "sandwich" named after Hillel
Has a taste that is much worse than even the smell.
But when that assault to your taste buds has ceased,
You'll claim your reward: It's now time for our feast!

Dinner

Following dinner, it may be difficult to recapture the attention of participants, particularly if there are a number of children present. The after dinner portion of the service is therefore purposely brief. It begins by harnessing excitement of the children, at least one of whom is anxiously awaiting their reward for having found the afikomen. The origin of the word is from the Greek "epikomonz" meaning dessert. The actual typically sweet dessert having already been eaten with dinner, it is logical to question why a piece of matzoh should be designated as dessert as well. The afikomen is a dessert only in the sense that it is the last bit of food eaten at a seder.

Leader rewards the finder(s) of the afikomen.

Leader may explain one rationale for this custom, seemingly somewhat out of place in such a solemn event as a seder: The Talmud is a profound, deeply introspective, and serious contemplative review, over sixty volumes in length, thoughtfully compiled over countless generations. In the Talmud, brilliant scholars and learned clergy propose philosophical interpretations of Jewish laws and customs. That same usually no-nonsense Talmud proposes the following in an atypically lighthearted, yet common sense based theory regarding the afikomen: The wise scholars simply propose that the anticipation of a reward for finding the afikomen, a ceremonial dessert without which the seder cannot be consummated, helps keep children awake and more attentive throughout the seder.

Prior to asking a participant to open a door for Elijah, Leader may explain why some feel that Elijah, a 9th century B.C. prophet, or messenger from God, is included in the ceremony. Many feel that Elijah is meant to give hope and inspiration to humanity before the biblical End of Days. At Leader's discretion, it may be wise to skip the alternate thoughts which follow: Another theory is that Elijah comes to check that every male participant is circumcised. Why should this matter? On the night that the tenth deadly plague ravaged the Egyptian firstborn, the angel of death delivering that God given decree bypassed only specially designated homes. Best known of that special designation was the lamb blood with which the Jews had been instructed to clearly mark their front door jambs. Less known is that the angel of death recognized that bloody demarcation only if the home was inhabited by circumcised males.

Participant opens a door for Elijah, the prophet.
Optional: Sing Eliyahu Hanavi

Leader concludes the service:

Now last, thanks again Lord, for fruit of the vine.
It colors our grape juice; the source of our wine.
The fourth cup of wine we'll combine with the third,
Since the hour is late, we condense now our words.

Blessing #5: Third and fourth cup of wine

אַתָּה יְיָ אֱלֹהֵינוּ מֶלֶךְ הָעוֹלָם בּוֹרֵא פְּרִי הַגָּפֶן.

Baruch Atah Adonai, Eloheinu melech ha'olam, borei p'ri hagafen.

We praise You, Adonai our God, Ruler of the Universe,
Who creates the fruit of the vine.

The story's been told: time to finish our talk.
We have opened the door, so Elijah can walk
Right up to our table, and share all our blessings;
And as we conclude, I must be confessing,
I've loved every minute together tonight,
And hope that conditions will someday be right
For peace to break out, with no reason to fight;
In Jerusalem we'll feast that magical night!

Optional songs at conclusion:

Chag Gadya
Dayenu
Hatikvah

Eliyahu Hanavi

אֵלִיָּהוּ הַנָּבִיא, אֵלִיָּהוּ הַתִּשְׁבִּי, אֵלִיָּהוּ הַגִּלְעָדִי. בִּמְהֵרָה
בְּיָמֵינוּ, יָבוֹא אֵלֵנוּ, עִם מָשִׁיחַ בֶּן־דָּוִד.

Eliyahu hanavi
Eliyahu hatishbi
Eliyahu, Eliyahu, Eliyahu, hagil'adi.
Bim'herah beyaneinu, yavo eleinu
I'm Mashi'ach ben David,
I'm Mashi'ach ben David.

English translation

Elijah the prophet
Elijah the Tishbite
Elijah the Giladite

May He soon, in our days, come to us
With the messiah son of David
With the messiah son of David.

Dayenu
Shortened version

אִלּוּ הוֹצִיאָנוּ מִמִּצְרַיִם, דַּיֵּנוּ.

Ilu hotzi, hotzianu, hotzianu miMitzrayim, hotzianu, miMitzrayim, Dayenu.

Chorus (to be sung after each main verse):

**Da dayenu, da dayenu, da dayenu, dayenu dayenu, dyenu,
Da dayenu, da dayenu, da dayenu, dayenu dayenu.**

אִלּוּ נָתַן לָנוּ אֶת־הַשַּׁבָּת, דַּיֵּנוּ.

Ilu natan, natan lanu, natan lanu et haShabbat, natan lanu, et haShabbat, Dayenu.

Chorus

אִלּוּ נָתַן לָנוּ אֶת־הַתּוֹרָה, דַּיֵּנוּ.

Ilu natan, natan lanu, natan lanu et haTorah, natan lanu et haTorah, Dayenu.

Chorus

English translation

Verse 1:
If He had brought us out of Egypt

Verse 2:
If He had given us the Shabbat

Verse 3:
If He had given us the Torah
Dayenu translates basically as
"That would have been enough."

Chad Gadya

Shortened Version

Chad gadya, chad gadya
Dizvan aba bit'rei zuzei
Chad gadya, chad gadya.

V'ata shunra v'achal l'gadya
Dizvan aba bit'rei zuzei
Chad gadya, chad gadya.

V'ata chalba v'nashach l'shunra.
Di achal l'gadya
Dizvan aba bit'rei zuzei
Chad gadya, chad gadya.

V'ata chutra v'hika l'chalba.
V'ata nura v'saraf l'chutra.
V'ata maya v'chava l'nura.
V'ata tora v'shata l'maya.
V'ata hashochet v'shachat l'tora.
V'ata Malach Hamavet v'shachat l'tora.
V'ata Hakadosh Baruch Hu
v'shachat l'Malach Hamavet

English translation

One little goat, one little goat
That my father bought for two zuzim.

One little goat, one little goat.

Along came a cat and ate the goat
That my father bought for two zuzim.

One little goat, one little goat.

Along came a dog
And bit the cat
That ate the goat
That my father bought for two zuzim.

One little goat, one little goat.

Along came a stick and beat the dog;
Along came a fire and burnt the stick;
Along came water and put out the fire;
Along came an ox and drank the water;
Along came a butcher and slaughtered the ox;
Along came the Angel of Death
and killed the butcher;
Along came the Holy One and
slew the Angel of Death.

Hatikvah

כָּל־עוֹד בַּלֵּבָב פְּנִימָה נֶפֶשׁ יְהוּדִי הוֹמִיָּה
וּלְפַאֲתֵי מִזְרָח קָדִימָה עַיִן לְצִיּוֹן צוֹפִיָּה.
עוֹד לֹא אָבְדָה תִקְוָתֵנוּ הַתִּקְוָה שְׁנוֹת אלפיים
לִהְיוֹת עַם חָפְשִׁי בְּאַרְצֵנוּ בְּאֶרֶץ צִיּוֹן בירושלים.

Kol od balevav p'nimah
Nefesh Yehudi homiyah.
Ulfa'atey mizrach kadimah Ayin l'tzion tzofiyah.
Ode lo avdah tikvatenu,
Hatikvah bat shnot alpayim,
L'hiyot am chofshi b'artzenu
B'eretz Tzion v'Yerushalayim.

English translation

As long as the Jewish spirit is yearning
Deep in the heart
With eyes turned toward the East,
Looking toward Zion,
Then our hope — the two-thousand-year-old hope
Will not be lost:
To be a free people in our land,
The land of Zion and Jerusalem.

Printed in the United States
by Baker & Taylor Publisher Services